A LETTER TO THE PRESIDENT

Poems

Mbizo Chirasha

Edited by Jabulani Mzinyathi

Cover art by Tendai Mwanaka

Mwanaka Media and Publishing Pvt Ltd,
Chitungwiza Zimbabwe
*
Creativity, Wisdom and Beauty

i

Publisher: Tendai R Mwanaka
Mwanaka Media and Publishing Pvt Ltd *(Mmap)*
24 Svosve Road, Zengeza 1
Chitungwiza Zimbabwe
mwanaka@yahoo.com
www.africanbookscollective.com/publishers/mwanaka-media-and-publishing
https://facebook.com/MwanakaMediaAndPublishing/

Distributed in and outside N. America by African Books Collective
orders@africanbookscollective.com
www.africanbookscollective.com

ISBN: 978-1-77906-499-8
EAN: 9781779064998

DISCLAIMER
All views expressed in this publication are those of the author and do not necessarily
reflect the views of *Mmap*.

TABLE OF CONTENTS

PART THREE

FOREWORD

Here is an eagle's eyes scanning beyond the boundaries of his native Zimbabwe to right the crookedness of men with dubious ideals and reckless twists in lands abroad. A man who has traversed the world on the wings of words, his first stint out was in 2003 as a team member of the young delegates of Zimbabwe writers to the land of the Fins. Caressing his Lenovo mistress upon a night, he relives in recorded poesy, memories of victims of corruption and the false memoirs of looters of the land. A letter to the PRESIDENCY, collection of his experimental poetry is such an outcome.

Here is THE man on a mission and with a mission. Words are slings and rocks on his quiver. Tireless and resilient; no ugliness is too ugly to stay below his radar. His weapon of choice is his pen. Dipped in acid, as he says, no thug escapes the roast of his laser beaht.ms that put them on the spotlight.

The man with letters that fly the uneven potholed roads of the African continent and beyond, uncloaking the masks of pretenders. Roads laced with skulls and the stench and fumes of the dying and dead. Roads where hyenas in smoky grey boardrooms suits determine the fate of masses weak and naïve. A man born in a place and stage when the time was ripe for his warrior spirit to spit on the burning issues with words that highlight the reason and seasons to heal the ills. A man among men with the whip of Jesus in the temple uncompromising at the cross of rebuke and crucifixion.

The man who sleeps uneasy at the molestation of a child. A man who boils with rage at the rape of a girl. A man who exposes the rot in society regardless of who the perpetrator is. His royalty is to truth and justice for all. His companion is ideas that better society. His heritage is fair play for all.

Mbizo Chirasha, is a poet's poet. A writer's writer. A king of words and a servant in one. One, hard to describe for he describes words. Here's a man hard to simplify.

Nancy Ndeke (POET , WRITER , EDUCATOR AND LITERARY ARTS ACTIVIST) from Kenya.

PART ONE

GOOD MORNING PRESIDENT

(i)

I saw Kaguta chasing ghost of Obote behind sand hills of Lahore. Mirisho carrying the shadows of Kambarage along footpath of Bangamoyo. Pythagoras and Mohamed fasting along the banks of Yamuna after a corruption binge in a Nollywood heart- throbber. Cappuccino mullahs and monks plucking wheat in bread land Punjab chanting sutra in a Hollywood blockbuster. Zapiro and Wangari slicing beetroot behind Shinto shrines in a Hollywood trailblazer. Archbishops and Kabbalists sharing oxygen with Janjaweed in temples of hongaji, faces buried in clouds of hashish and bhudhists incense mist.

(ii)

I am a poet with nostalgia of innocence. My pen is dipped in acid to burn revolutions that roast voters in political ovens. My poetry is my energy charging me like battery. I respect no test-tube presidents whose political Embryos are raised in boardroom populism. Whose political fetus are fed by newsroom evangelism. While cities are choked to death by explosions. Statesmen born out of political emotions than elections.

(iii)

African statesmen enjoy oxmopurcino in gardens of Riviera. Dancing the
breeze of vineyards. Sipping from expensive glasses of English wine. Rocked
by beetles invented pop and Pier rick Pedron American style jazz in opera-de
Paris. Their state houses decorated with diamond arts of Picasso and Lorenzo
lotto. Antananarivo   and Wagadugu blighted by sufferings. Radio Latina
flighting dramatic footages of African doldrums nothing brightening. The
horizons of black townships buried in smoldering ruins. Kiberia, broken
limps dancing in teargas and water cannons. Admirals and pseudo generals
wielding pangas in dandora slums. Moslems of Mombasa blown sideways by
the wrong whirlwind of islamophobia. Bring us nanobitas of democracy not
shigellas of autocracy.

SLUM DOGS AND PROPAGANDA JACKALS

(i)

Patriots stinking propaganda leprosy. Corruption exploding bellies of
economic Tsars. Political vultures snaking on media propaganda of the
demise of the prince of Pozarevac. Milosevic planting suicide grenades in
fields of ruin. Bullets sprinkling blood in burning villages. Leaving traces of
wounded memories in Haditha. Shanty towns bathing in water cannons and
breathing teargas. Refugees carrying burden of sorry memories their children
born out of double revolutions. Revolutions of blood graffiti and propaganda
literati,

(ii)
Children eating bitter fruits of times. Serpents celebrating new rhythms of
slave trade. Blood rivers flooding funeral slums of Lima
youngsters taught to salute dead comrades with famine
riddled slogans. War pounding the doors of Darfurians. Widows intoxicated
by doctrines of martyrdom. Bring Raisa, Christina and Evita to exorcise
demons of political pimping. Bring Shakespeare and Chekhov to eulogize
dead victims and heroes. Victims of propaganda ideology and blood theology.
Heroes of freedom discord.

(iii)
Our times are wounded by nosema and shigella
in prostitute's slums and corruption streets
bring Nefertiti the princess of pyramids not stomach wrenching slogans of
Osama. I see Musharraf reading toxic poetry to Sharif. Good morning
Vietnam. Good morning Guantanamo. Good morning Pakistan

(iv)

11

We are hunger blown hyenas in torn leather bikinis. Siting at the bottom with red eyes like bullets ready to clutch fatty backs of big elephants above. Gossip mongers whose empty bellies stuffed with Propaganda ice-blocks and bitter political grapes. We have lost our salt. Minds dieting on Facebook Fanta and Google pizza

LETTER TO REVOLUTIONS

(i)
I am a poet born out of freedom slums. Freedom germinating into poverty. I am the stench and drench of Karantina village. I am the martyr exploding metaphoric cyanide in operation Bonjika.Satirist breakfasting from imams, mullahs, rabbis, monks and ayatollahs in the holy city of Najaf. I sing of the ghost of Bagdad regaining lost pride. I am the spirit of Isheguro vulgarizing aristocrats. I cry with villages of Sewa.I weep with dry but oil soaked streets of Mosul

(ii)
I am not foul smelling semen of ruffians
I am not a slice of oral history. I sing of gun rhythms of Hiskanita. I sing of orange revolutions congested by cigar butts and rifle butts. I sing of Ollanta and Ortega. I sing of Kitchener and Tabare. I am not the stench of xenophobia in the Divasdero. I weep of generations after Arafat. I sing of Michelle and Lula. I am not a poet born out of sexual revolutions. I sing of songs of Google and rough hymns KGB. I am not narco-dollars smelling shit. I sing of Castro drunk with communism. I sing of Chavez toxic with revolutionarism. Bring me Annan and Wangari . Bring Achebe to sing Things fall Apart and Ngugi to rewrite the Devils on the Cross .Bring ballot vases of Fiji.

(iii)
Sing Zeddillo. Sing Vicente. Sing Vaira. See Hafez burning Assad in the slums of Syria. Refugees toiling in Sheba farms. Pistol toting kids slicing Chatila. Bring Picasso and his pencils for blood washed Moluccas islands. Sing Hugo, sing Zamora to reap souls of Halmahera.

(iv)
I was born when Slobodan waved goodbye to Saddam,

Saddam waving back to Slobodan. I was born when century's conspiracy pogroms crucified torijos and Jaime. After the heart beating obituaries of Allende and Sukarno. Freedom messiahs Kwame and Lumumba kissed their rifles and bibles goodbye. **I was born** when the Groot krokodil prayed for the miracle of the Rainbow Nation to canvas genocide blisters. Africa is tired of reaping sweet bitter strawberries

(v)

I don't sing rhythms of rifles with verbal bravado. I am a poet telling hard truth. I sing not of bullies robbing our engines of their steam. I sing not of buddies diluting culture in the name of civilization. I am wizard of pen. My weapon drip with acid ink not human blood

ELDERS AND ELDERESSSES

(i)
Ghettoes sitting on burning composites. Political bed hoppers rubbing their noses in diplomatic shit. Justice taught to eagles in trees. Slogan fraudsters robbing praise from morphine-fuelled youth
And marijuana doped youngsters. Dissidents reaping blood dollars from stinking banking malls.

(ii)
Racism poisoned wells of our dignity
Tribalism, Pandemic soiling linen of humanity
I see imams burning Baptist bibles. Mafia rubbing blood on robes. Empress Nagako and Emperor Hirohito boarding political train of grey beards with Chancellor of Oxford, Duke of Connaught and Prince 11 of Monaco through the forbidden city of Tiananmen to the Skandia vale slums
Singing tunes with the archbishop of Chichele at the ritual ceremony with memories of Yokozuna and Plato.

(iii)
Writing epitaphs of long gone warriors and martyrs with Madame-de-Montville and the mafia laureate Lalita. Memoirs of Napoleon and Kaiser Willem. I sing of DE-radicalization of jihadists. Jihadist's of Reberalta. And home towns of Jeolla.Painting ballot vases crimson red
One day Hindu saints and Anglican vicars share a tub of conscience. Pontiffs and mullahs shall swig juices in decency. Rabbis and ayatollahs burn frankincense

(iv)
Villages breeding dissidents. Corrupted by bearded lunatics of camp Peddleton. Pontiffs and sheiks fighting over beaurucratized political pulpits,

after years of political arithmetic. Mahindra and Synedria singing sutra in
camps of scheme. Danube hazing in drugs and alcohol
Pakistan a country of scheme. Nepal a country of famine
Good morning princess Infanta Dona Margarita. Good morning
commandant Castro. Melinda the Queen of Microsoft. Picasso the Village
boy of Basque. Good afternoon detainees and generals. Good afternoon coup
d'états and corrupted innocents.

PAPARRAZZI PIZZA

(i)
Paparazzi field day in La Dolce Vita. Blowing their noses with propaganda
cocaine. Painting their blood with slogan nicotine. Waiters serving condoms
and cucumbers. Blood cannot be corrupted. Blood hold the secrets of
belonging. I sing of juntas, sneezing coup-de-tats tonsillitis. Dictators
suffering from autocratic hepatitis. Remember the gore soaked soil of
Mesopotamia. King Abdul-Aziz reciting Koran after suicide bombs. Goofies
drinking warm waters of the gulf. Taliban warlords roasting Jude rein souls in
religious ovens. Strong political brew from Greek islands of Samos. Cultural
elites and Baptist, zealots, monks, and elders singing sutra to slum dwellers
after the roses and blood. Remember, robbed the soul to Benazir

(ii)
I can hear voices of ayatollah and Sheik Hasina, their lips dripping with
sorrow. Patel's and kolis freezing in the cold island of Pentecost. Abdulla
eating chicken curry in glitterati dinner with Bangladesh after a diplomatic
mix. Ghost of Wilson and shadows of Clinton bathing together in humiliation
tub. Before going down with the sinking sun. Bring the spy craft combat that
I drink espresso with stasis, sip
Cappuccino with KGB. Shop with Mossad from posh malls of Bole Road.
Bring me the creative oxygen of Obama. Royalty robes of Madiba. I see wild
dogs tearing democracy apart. Red ants digging into the spine of the
economy. Politics stinking like old urine. Puppets eating lollies. Stooges
sucking lollipop. Evita smashing beetroot. Zille chewing African potato

BLOOD PETALS

(i)
I see villagers in Hebbel digging own graves. Rot of mobo-crats. Autocrats decaying villages into slums in the name of ideology. Stalin students flashing morals in pit latrines. Hitler pals dragging freedom to Golgotha. Our sweat deodorizing hard revolutions in sugar mills and cocoa fields. Flags blowing away freedom in Saundati state of Karantaka. Teargas spray painting revolutions in ghetto cities of Belford Roxo.

(ii)
When will Rwanda drown the sand dunes of genocide?
While others still steal African sunlight with African holocaust
Serengeti is for Wodaaba. Kenya is for Kenyatta.
I am not Ogun the god of iron and the road. I am not sarowiwa the martyr of Ogoni. Not Abacha, the butcher of Abuja drunk with blood. Not Kuti the populist of afro-verses. Not Okoti the poet of Ocoli songs. I am the griot of our times. Bring water gourds to wet seedbeds of revolution. Propaganda our addiction. Condoms our diction
Guns have long taken our manhood. Bring the angel of Soweto to sing Mbaqanga of Amandla.Freedom!

(iii)
Bullets smashing infants' bladders in Fallujah. Grinding mothers intestines in Bullets Island. Propagandist waving burning flags Jalalabad. Mothers harvesting corpses like cotton balls at dawn. Villagers breathing cordite in Kazastan. Bring beccari and Fangarrezi big batkas of Vatican to loosen the conveyor belts of radicals. Bring seminarians and saints to glisten bellies of children with cocoa butter.

WALKING GHOSTS

(i)
Who will visit Mekong delta of shrimp with princes and sultans? Vietnam is heiroglyficed with blood graffiti. Serbia doing the last shahada after dirty bombs. Drug barons swinging in bling of Las Vegas, walking through the scar of shame. Eating paella and dancing sangria. See Wiranto and Kambada playing golf in islands of Sumatra. Ernesto chasing the shadow of Fujimori in the sands of panama.Sukano and Suharto jiving for freedom in Virgin Islands during the month of Ramadan. Bibi dancing with Mafia in Princess Hotel before Yonge Street. Benedict of Nurcia grabbing sun from Osama of Torabora in the streets of Samawa

(ii)
Tears graffiti scrawled on debris of pentagon. Smell of smoldering walls smashing through September sunset. Tower of Juche still stands Karalla. Portraits of Susilo and Zapatero are compasses to the streets of elections, which flow with blood. We are tired of extremists in jackets of peaceniks. Dogs barking corruption behind banking castles. Dissident presidents wearing berets not helmets reaping corpses from war fields.

BREAKFASTING BULLETS

(i)
Beggar ghosts walking in the smoke of burning dagga in Kalinga-linga.
Corruption shopping in fluorescent malls of Kabulonga. Abidjan mother's
breast feeding test tube born children. Kindergartens sucking grenades for
breasts. Lawyers bribed by despots whose fingertips itch with compatriot's
blood. Racism is the blight of the tomatoes of our conscience. Xenophobia is
sepsis against freedom. Freedom grinding under the remote control of
propaganda machinery,
De-Moslemization of Asia
Bleeding wounds of Turkmenistan
Shrieking souls of Uzbekistan

(ii)
I am not a baby born with a dead tongue. I am a xylophone to welcome
ghosts from battle fields. See flags waving good morning to death. I will sing
my poems to Isomura, Mayor of Osaka. Cross bridges of injustice with
Rolihlahla. Board the freedom train with Yolanda King. Sit for dinner with
Vilma, Hayashida of Kyoto. Anglican nuns and knights of Dagama.

RAINBOWS AND WHIRLWINDS

(i)
Comeback Ameriya and Ardhamiya. Sing for the golden doomed shrine of
Samara. Bullet leaves traces like semen. Remember the battle of Fallujah.
Vietnamese pimping stores of pimps smoking newspaper rolled Imboza,
death of Martyrs and monks of Arandinga in Zaragoza, in the name of
dictablanda.Bring the scribes of Mauritania, the Indian island state of Africa
Bring scribes from Sukhothai
Bring scribes from clubs of Soho
Media is the barometer to measure political pressure. Thermometer to
measure to measure temperature of democracy. Rain-gauge to measure
dampness of plutocracy. Bring Tata Mandela and the Ethiopian eunuch for
we are writhing in hovels of slavery and bible. Africa is not the doormat of
the west to wipe off blood of Bagdad and Arabia. Africa rise, rise Africa from
the bitter past of Columbus, Dagama and Rhodes.
Sing Salif Keita! Sing Fodoba, Sing Sokoni Kante, Sing Fela Kuti. Sing!

A DANCE OF MADNESS

(i)
Dictators leave fingerprints on coffee mugs and footprints on red carpets.
Tears of mothers dripping grenade dowsed corpses. Corridors of Power
littered with political corpses. In villages suffocating under propaganda
stamina and blood lust riflemen
Slum fontanel's boiling in the sun of dissies from movement slums. Tired of
gun sound and abortion

(ii)
Come pempero wankulu
Come nomzano
Come Xhwahu Lengweni
Come resurrect hawker-filled streets of Joslovo and Khayelitsha,
Of mothers sacrificed on the altar of ambition. Come Tata to end stomach
turning gun thunders of Kokoarangana
Blood culture of hashish syndicates in the port of smugglers.
Bonaparte and Amini hugging in a dictator's concert. Eating granadilla lollies
and chicken mayonnaise in Kore Blixen coffee garden. Children in
Dayapetrovic camp seduced by mindless sperm dispensers. King Abdullah
and mama supping porcinis mushroom at La pentola en-route to Island Of
kolombongara. Banning the bitter past of arabesques and sheikdoms

(iii)
Our destiny can no longer determined by flags blowing away our past. We
are children born out burning suns of Sahara and hot sands of Kalahari.
Citizens whose sweat is gulped by land barons and land baroness in sugar
islands of Galapagos. We belong to the streets of Hargeisa, Bonino and
Saramago.Media wagons hot blazing with vulgar and racial bile. Bring me to
the state of Tabasco to drink red wine with Madrazo and sheik khalifa.
Walking along in the pollution city of Amarillo

(iv)

Do we belong here? The womb of our past sage with souls of martyrs and freeedomites silenced by phlegm of exploitation. Epitaphs written by Google. Funeral dirges ritualized in Hollywood glitterati. We are dogs eating cucumbers for breakfast and condoms for supper. Slaves of sugar and blood. Children of genocided villages, never fondled breasts of our beauties but licked the blood of our mothers. Drunk with slogan cocaine and political slavery in slums. Slums killed by mobile phones and Walkman's. Slums robbed of their diamond through bible rhymes and live bullets

CONTRADICTIONS

(i)
We are martyrs of deportation
Orphans of organized economic agenda
Children born out of social vendetta. Our father is sanctions
Mother corruption. Stepmother inflation

Racially defamed. Colonially handicapped

See our professors dishing out their intellectual omelet in faculties of Oxford
and Harvard. While their dusty ridden streets hungry of intellectual
drumsticks.
Villagers depleted by apartheid syphilis. Cities drown in social thrombosis

(ii)
Africa. A contrast
Poverty the jingle of citizens. See the bottoms of city of gold
.See bucket latrines. Townships smelling sadness. Chinization of Africa

Violence, our disease. Racism, a pandemic
Xenophobia is endemic. Blood spilling is epidemic.

IAM THE VOICE OF RENNAISANCE

(i)

Tears graffiti scrawled on the debris of Pentagon. Smell of smoldering walls smashing through September sunset. Tower of Juche still stand like Kearala. Portraits of susilo and zapatero are compasses to the streets of elections that flow blood. We are tired of extremists in jackets of peaceniks. Dogs barking corruption behind banking castles. Dissident presidents wearing berets instead of helmets reaping corpses from war fields. I am not a child of pleasant memories. I cry of bombing of Zalambesa by pangarist. I am not a poet of yakuza. I am not a product of super power summits. I am the voice of renaissance. I am the heartbeat of freedom

(ii)

Rhythm of my voice is bottled in the marrow of the state
Tongue of the moon kissed the bullet fractured skin of the night
Fingers of the sun caress the machete sliced bosoms of horizon
Smell of apartheid linger on the thighs of rainbow nation
Stink of discrimination bottled in brand of reconciliation
I am the candlelight against the nights of stigmatization
I am a griot erasing shadows of marginalization. I am a poet waving for glocalization

(iii)

I am a patriot of words revolution. Lyrical depth of Shakur. Poetic breath of Maya Angelou. Descendant Langston Hughes metaphors
Identity rhythm of Senghor. I am afro pop. The rhythm of Keita and Kuti, Masekela rhymes. Makeba song of freedom. I bubble with consciousness. Whirlwind of renaissance. I am epitaph of widows in Rwanda. Silenced

Congo. Orphaned Darfur. Plundered Burundi. Sanctioned Zimbabwe. My freedom Boeing 707 is Martin Luther King. My freedom train Malcolm Little X
My freedom spear is Bantu Biko, Spear of the Nation. I am a literary brothel condomized with words

STATE OF THE NATION ADRESS

 I see dreams of this country floating in the stench of
bubbling Sewer Rivers. Poverty shriveled chests of mother's luggage sorrow
baggage. Sorrows blooming like flowers every season

Mothers cutting the freedom cake,
with aluminum tears foiled faces. Children munching the freedom,
cream with poverty rugged yellow maize teeth

Fathers celebrating with election chopped arms. Ministers Mercedes convoys
swimming in highway potholes. Corruption, the Vaseline polishing the floor
of state.

Flowers of Justice died with last decade sinking sun. Daughters eat political
regalia like omelet for breakfast,
sons munching torn soot laden diplomas for supper. Peasants sniffing the
smell of the rotting sun. Voters enjoying the catchy perfume of propaganda
again,
mentally sodomized

The scars of the last season are the signature of the next election. Wounds of
last winter bloom another pain in this winter. Diggers of the truth bring me
jugs filled with lemon juice of justice. I am drunk with barrels of orange
bitterness

Freedom is the placard on your chest. Democracy is how you shake your fist.
Mother sing me true freedom songs
erase these wounds opened in the charcoal of violence,
machetes signatured leadership name tags on our mother's breasts. Pink bras
coughing blood beside ballot boxes
bullets wrote epitaphs for funerals of children unlimited
black cockerels drinking black eggs in dying winter nights,

black nights. Acid of politics bleaching the trust of the flag. Its sacred colors melting in the lotion of grief,

Bring me the sneeze of Murenga. Download the cough of Nehanda from her chest
blow the wind into the shrine of Munhumutapa,

Godfathers of change breakfasted muffins of change. Bathing with same bath-soap in froth-filled tubs of corruption .See the red, yellow, orange, chameleon colors in the East. I smell the foul breath of sanctions from the West. Paparazzi smiling to the bank after sprees of recycled headlines. I am a poet born in grapevines of colonial bitterness and groomed in apple grooves of factional hatred,

Light for me bright candles for another satire,
to fry fat cats in oil pans of metaphors and repent crude mobsters into true revolutionaries

MY POETRY

My poetry is bitter breakfast of propaganda-crats
My poetry is grenade planted in the hearts of corruption-crats. It is an enzyme
of justice, fermenting potbellies of fat cats. Diet for PhDs with theories of
Fanon and Malcomx. Reason of freedom sipped from revolutionary coffee
cups

My poetry

Is sanguaged between 1980 and 1966. It is medulla of voters drunk with their
blood. Metaphor of greenhorns drunk with ambition.an oxymoron of Osama
and Obama. Haiku of gushungo, madiba and Nkrumah. A sonnet of
Vietnam, Baghdad, pentagon, afghan, Taliban, Congo, Darfur
Rwanda, Soweto, Sharpeville, Georgia and Tele-Aviv

My Poetry

It is a hyperbole of Bagdad scarlet and Sharpeville crimson
It is a ballad of Nefertiti, Nandi, and Nehanda, Pompano and Maphela.
Nzinga and other prophetesses. It is the last wail of Saddam, Slobadan,
Bokasa, Dada, Abacha, babanginda and Ngwazi

My poetry

It is an obituary of samora, fanon, kuti, Luther, sarowiwa, kimathi, Hani,
mahlangu, tongogara.Juxtaposition of pagan and Christian. Parody of
characters dancing 1994 genocide musical. A farce of stooges of bread slices
and tea.
Bitter sarcasm of hunger crushing tummies of ballot tired peasants and juntas

"TRIBUTE TO AFRICAN WRITERS"

 I wrote so long a letter to Mayombe and Anowa.That will marry when I want. For the beautiful ones are not yet born.
While we wait for the rain .In the coming of the dry season. Behind the anthills of savannah. Milking the cows of Shambati, gathering good bits of wood and the fortunes of Wangarini.

In that forests of a thousand demons. A sleep walking land, for things had fallen apart. We faced the wrath of the ancestors, bones and shadows. For it was not any easy walk to freedom
With farai girls, nehanda and the son of the soil. In that long journey of popynongena.We met Matigari,
And the tycoon from Peter Maritz burg. The poor Christ of Bomba. We saw the devil dangling on thecross ,
We had he arrows of God,
We wanted to kill the mangy dog. In the river between was this a war of freedom? Indaba my children
We sang the song of la-wino and Ocol.Walking down Second Avenue.
Fighting to decolonize the minds of the people,
We became the house of hunger, In the country of our own
The butterfly was burning. In the burning summer season,
We never ate the grain of wheat .For we harvested thorns
And nervous conditions. Cry my beloved country. Country of my skull. For Nevada still snores. Even after the struggle of Zimbabwe.

DEMOCRACY

Democracy is not stomached in silencers and machine guns of Klux Klux Klan, Triple K. It is not contained in cargos of ARV and condoms dispatched to black villages and Philippine hamlets in the name of HIV mitigation. Not blood grants donated to Kibera and Soweto in the name of poverty alleviation. Not freedom castrating other freedoms. Blunt propaganda machetes circumcising political toddlers

(ii)
Democracy! Democracy is not gun totting brigades. Gun saluting militia. Not globe-trotting ministers. Deafening whistles of motorcades. Not mobutu.habre, abacha, bokasa, polpot, Caligula. Not in the fontanel's of political gods. Portraits of leaders who died with blood on their hands. Democracy is not lyrics of funky, punkie music from ghetto fabulous. In the hotbunsexselling magazines on Hollywood lamppost. Not the storylines of MTV. Headlines of BBC.Nationalism infested ZBC.Communism gobbled ATV. Western diluted BTV. AND many other super bulletins you know about.

(iii)
Democracy! Democracy is not the rehabilitation of Kirikiri and Robin Island prisons. Rainbownization of South Africa. Dirty commerce at the Kazungula, Port Mombasa and Port Harcourt. Not numbers of spoiled ballots and scars of bullets. Skin pigmentation of controversial martyrs. Democracy is not cannibals roasting of crawling revolutions. Not warlords breakfasting bullets shells drinking blood for cappuccino. Warlord eating broken limps for hamburgers. Atomic bombs coughing blood in pubs of Baghdad. Hydrogen bombs sneezing blood in pit latrines of Hiroshima. Petrol bombs vomiting war in temples of Gaza strip and synagogues of Lebanon

(iv)
Democracy! Democracy is not Marxist ideologies. Not principles of
our republics. Not contained in the blood juice of orange style
revolutions. In the chlorophyll of green revolutions. Not in the blisters
of Prince Tafari Mackinnon inflicted by oppressive dans. Democracy is
not rewriting African culture with an English instinct. Zulunization of
Methodist priests. Burning incense in Popedomes. Wind choking
hymns of faith mission congregants. Legalized sharia commandments
in mosques

(v)
Democracy. Democracy is not the right side of the inflation blighted
coin. Bible verses written in graffiti in street gutters. Not propaganda
cinnamoned podiums. Not Jamaican poetess drugged by reggae
poetries. Not heart piercing teachings white phobia. Soul burning
teachings of blackphobia. Mind blasting culture of xenophobia.
Demoracry! Democracy is democracy!

PART TWO

(1).
Robots are dead and the City is blind
People are holding on half-baked hopes.
Streets are dark. Mothers weep from teargas sting.
Robots are dead. Presidents are drinking our hopes for wine
Streets are sneezing poverty. Ministers cuddle their potbellies in whisky
taverns
Villages are coughing hunger. Parliament adjourned to send a befitting
farewell to a dead money launder.
Robots are dead. Congress celebrates an autocrat with fun and pomp
City is blind. Robots are dead

(2).
Promises eaten in super-glittering motels. Hopes stripped naked in red
light wine bars. Republic manifestos scribbled in corridor brothels.
Election boxes calculated in crank stores. Rope of violence suffocating
my country to death. True revolutionaries freezing in ideological cold-
rooms. Fake patriots drinking the rich revolutionary brew. Paedophiles
salivating to masturbate on the succulent bosom of the new republic.
Madness!

(3)
I was born along with this country. Listening the afro beat of politics.
Fist of slogans smashing into mother's faces. Sisters raped in the reggae
of propaganda. Sons dancing to the funk music of violence. Bathing
villages in blood. I was born along with this country. Listening to the
afro beat of political music.

(4)
A country thirsty of freedom. Burning in pans of hepatitis and poverty.
We sniff the smell of apartheid with heavy hearts. Aroma of

xenophobia choking city nostrils. Stench of violence suffocating villagers

(5)
I see mothers in the train to another Rhodesia. Wincing after fist blows by the New Republic. Shrieking in the pain of their return to dark past. Laughter of drums is long gone with blowing winds

(6)
My village packed a powerful poetry meal. A drum beat. A wail from thirsty patched throats of peasants waiting for another hope. A wail for freedom

(7)
Paparazzi breakfast toast bread of your name
Your totem is their coffee
Cartoonists pitch favelas on your face
They will even follow you in your way to hell.

(8)
The chamber is full of cannibals. Eating dreams of the people. Munching the hope of our mothers. Garnishing the flesh of the country. Drinking up the passion of the state with ambition.

(9)
We were all born here in this darkness. Quilted by the pale shadow of sunshine city. Sodden with tears of fake patriots and stale sweat of tired citizens,

(10)
Devils are harvesting gems. Masses eating fear.
Mad devils reaping gold. Daughters embracing chaff.

(11)
We last giggled in 1980
The country lost its dimples in 1990
We lost our smiles during 2000sunset
Villages are angry. Streets are coughing disease,

(12)
I walked many miles in the desert of hope
My ashes of ambition are now cold
I am carrying buckets of sand in my soul
I need an orange juice of freedom!

(13)
We tired of gulping diluted ideological brew. This earth is barren of
justice. Villages are wet with cheap propaganda. Shrieking under the
burden of hope smashing fist slogans

(14)
Motorcade WAILS blown away your love of the people
Whirlwinds chased your soul away from the masses
Peasants are waiting for your return.
CHEF!

(15)
Satire is my DNA
Bring me threads of metaphor to stitch the rags of the country
together.
A country torn into tatters by paradox and hyperbole.

(16)
I was born in the winter of this country. My fontanels drilled by the
clutter of the gun. A country born out of the sound of the black

cockerel. The beat of the reggae drum. Black cockerel is now silent. The beat of the drum is long gone with the mist of cheap gossip.

(17)
The streets are drunk with heroin. Slumlords pimping daughters for ganja. Gangsters baptising sons in crack and Skokian. Slums sneezing poison. Fat cats farting blood diamonds.

(18)
Our mothers are now poverty addicts. We are babies of drought relief and GMOS. Corruption flow in the bone and marrow of the state. Scandal is in its DNA

(19)
I was not born with a silver spoon in my dimples. I was born with a golden pen in my hand. My pen is a weapon of mass instruction urinating bullets on corruption dinner tables.

(20)
Stale sweat never washed memories,
Memories of Madiba and Robben Island
Memories of Biafra and its past
Of sarowiwa and Ogoniland

Bitter tears never washed memories
Memories of Kimathi and bitterness
Memories of Bantu biko and tears
Memories of Nehanda and her bones

Split blood never washed the memories
Memories of Murenga and Chimurenga
Memories of Nyadzonia and the gun
Memories of Soweto and Sarafina

Memories!

(21)
VIVA PRESIDENT VIVA! VIVA REPUBLIC VIVA!

Viva Peasants Viva, Viva! I found my voice in the reggae of satire
I am the black poet with a black catholic president

Viva patriots' Viva, Viva. Viva Azania Viva. I want to finish my next
poem. A Metaphor with filaments of liberty

Viva Zambezi Viva. Viva Republic Viva. I grew up in the marrow of
this country. Dancing to the blues of peasants. And the jazz of city
labourers

Viva President Viva.Viva Azania VIVA!
I watched this country in excruciating pangs of pain .I see heaving
souls
Viva Patriots Viva! I found my voice in the afro beat of paradox.
Voters nodding to new blank political tunes
Viva president Viva. Viva Republic Viva!

(22)
Masses are holding to the manifesto with absent minds. Pangs of
hunger eating their bellies. People carried the republic in their hard fists
in turbulent seasons. I am writing this paradox to the masses of hunger
scorched peasants .Petit Stalinists who breakfast the bullet for omelette.
Masses are holding on to the manifesto with hunger twisting their tired
souls. Manifesto wet with bitter tears. Reeking with stale sweat of
hungry crop farmers.

(23)

I met this country early in life. Its dimples glowing with the passion of
a new revolution
Smiles of the republic hot with ambitions of patriots. Today .I am lost
in the dimness of a broken state

(24)
I see them children of the PoVo. Sitting on the rubble of their hovels.
Homeless.
Mangy dogs licking their bare bottoms. Gore dripping flags waving
goodnight to ballot duped cheerleaders.

(25)
Children licking palms of poverty with calculated gusto! In the name of
the Republic. Poets and laureates freeze in political cold-rooms
 Like sausage for another ballot breakfast.

(26)
A revolution is the aspiration of the masses. A revolution!
A revolution is not fiction. Not a faction!
It is not the soprano of the gun. It is the hit song of the people!

(27)
We sip your name from the brown tavern bottles
Potent brew carrying us to another day. Munching the flesh of your
totem for supper. You lost your salt. Mothers shriek in corrugated
hovels,
Drinking cold water with stale bread.

(28)
Wind of your breath switches off the country lights into dimness.
Sending streets to sleep before time. Wizards pimping gem fields' to
gluttonous imbeciles for imported rifles. Poverty hatching eggs in
pockets of parliament's overalls .Breeding hermits and urchins in the

hazy of corrupted malt whisky bottles. Breathe of the country reek the stink of old booze .Imbeciles reciting corruption footprints on state red carpets. Revolutionary rejects cheering dictator's fingerprints on ballot boxes. Political witches fornicating our national rhythm for peanut and ethanol.

(29)
I see you perched in latest convoys. Wives dancing in new reggae of slogans
Villagers stretching for the last Presidential T-shirt gift
Shefu----- Shefu ...

(30)
On this land of red millet
They water our dreams with tears. We are drinking the stale brew of freedom. Itch of poverty sits under our skin like syphilis.

(31)
As they reap motorcades and wealth. We all went to sleep half satisfied. After drinking the wind of empty slogan. With cheap propaganda biscuits.

(32)
My country chokes with poets. Underground Poets. Slam Poets. Academia and Zealots
Their rhymes failed to convince the president
Their breath stinks with cheap brew. Lips crack with propaganda ganja

(33)
I saw our flags signing the signature of freedom. Signature waving goodbye to poverty.
Now! Still Xenophobia eats supper with us.

Xenophobia drinking our anthems. Swallowing the dignity our emblems.

(34)
Stray dogs bark to our tattered dignity
Paparazzi coughing political-nicotined gossip
State sneezing teargas into dark streets choking our dignity to death

(35)
We fought for the land. We got the land
The land is vast. Dim robots rear our children,
  With dark streets breeding disease

(36)
Vendetta is burning the overalls of the state. Hatred peeling off parliament walls. We are walking like lost sheep. Mr GOVERNMENT, where are you

(37)
Citizens are watching the drama series. They are cooking answers in the pots of their souls. The seeds of liberation rose with the sun. Mothers watered the revolution with buckets of sweat. Children of the struggle still drink from jugs of tears. The revolution is frying daughters for supper.

(38)
Fat cats are drinking corruption drugs. Politicians munching sanction pills. Daughters hunting syphilis in red light district brothels. Babies suckling on dry and parched nipples. Our story is a bad story.

(39)
We shriek in the dimness of our hovels every night,

Anopheles drinking our last hope. We swallowed enough bitterness.
Our hearts are seething with hate. Blood boiling violence. We are fat
with your sweet talk
Poverty

(40)
Our mothers feed on wild berries. Termites and gossip their song. We
last sang the rain song long ago. We are children of drought relief and
gutter slang.

(41)
Cabinet tables are red with sweet wines. Streets boiling in raw sewage
Children eating diarrhoea .Drinking cholera,
 Parliaments talking vendetta! Mr President. I can't sing you for my
supper. I can't sing you for my breakfast
I will munch the ballot and swallow grenades. Peep through broken
windows of life. See ministers sipping our tears for breakfast.
Munching drumsticks of our dreams. Our hopes frozen in cold rooms
for the next political supper.

(42)
See cruel hands selling the country for ice sugar and cigars.

Cruel minds scheming genocide and snipe. Peace laureates relegated to
spectator terraces. Revolution hijacked.

Executive red carpets wet with borrowed ideological urine. A
bastardized revolution.

Mad morons urinating bombs in corridors of the country. Genocidal
imbeciles.
 People sipping new political concoctions. Faking satisfaction.

Zealots pimping this country for automatics and booze .Revolutionary rejects.

Gambling people in the chess of power game. Kleptomania.

(43)

We dreamt our dreams in gutter hovels. You eat them on parliament tables.

Cannibals

Our sweat is your hot cappuccino during cabinet talks.

Parasites

We breathe the shrapnel of your fart after you wash down your supper dinners with our bitter tears.

Hyenas

We pick the smithereens of your belch for breakfast.

Vultures!

(44)

They waited for you like at train station.

You didn't arrive

Sunburnt. Hunger smitten. Dancing to the war drumbeat like during Pungwes.

Mothers.

They waited for you patiently. Chanting old bush time songs.

Comrades.

They waited like in rain season. You didn't come!

You lost them in the sweet moan of your motorcade. **Patriots.**

They waited for you like in struggle .You didn't come

You lost them in the skyward heave of your helicopter. **Peasants.**

They waited for you forever and you didn't come!

(45)
We sang the new anthem. New flag
And the new black cockerel,
We danced for dawn and the Black cockerel
But---------------

PART THREE

VOLCANO

Mothers reaping tears in red-light streets. Rearing corpses in villages of
dust and birth. Harvesting nothing but dirges and cemeteries
Mothers do not tell when darkness end. Death written bon tired faces
and painted in dark walls of memories
Of those crucified by loss
Hear, a million footsteps rushing from one to another funeral dirge
Babies sucking from grief scorched nipples.

LETTER FROM HAITI

Black sister whose blood flow in my veins,
My wounds are your blister that boils with the fear of tomorrow and
yesterday
My sister in dust, in bullets, in freedom and flowers
I am the daughter of the moon and dust shipped up to hear by the boat
that missed bullets.

SONG OF GUYANA

Guyana
Raised through bowls of sweat in millet acres journeyed through
forests bullet shells and wounded dust,
Guyana is not the mist of forgotten and tired centuries. Guyana is the
succulent breast that dripped milk. Petal whose scent perfumed the
stink of the revolution

ARROWS OF RAYS

Gallant sun rays spring out of the womb of hills
Awakening villages from night of slumber
Soon clouds would roll and rain
Women with free and waiting breasts like detainees in dockyards turn
fresh cow heart brown clay in lush green fields of wheat
Milk plastered lips of babies tired in low rays of afternoon suns
Soon frogs will chant again and rhythm of nature will sing in pastures
again

THEIR HANDS

I passed through their hands
I can't tell how pricking and how caressing
With their odor of dead drunk democracy
Their hard metal autocracy stenciled on our slum walls
Their fingernails itching with greed

TOWNSHIP JUNCTION

I can see grenades loaded with dreams. Dreams of dying pavements
Dreams of bereaved streets. Euphoria of funeral songs emanating from
grave gardens
A plethora of scrap shovels lined up to mingle dead and dust.
Dreams dressed in denims and condom adverts. Dreams boiling in clay
pots. Dreams roasted in factory monoxides
Dreams entombed in bruised ululations and parched whistles

DAWN OF SUNSET

Laughter is long drained in our faces
Tired laden feet trudge through debris burning pavements
Our babies licking their parched lips for decade long
We are laborers who planted melons of freedom but never feasted
from their sweetness
Whose crest fallen breasts and shrunk nipples battled in many seasons
of want

DIARY OF AN ECONOMIC REFUGEE.

I have eaten my poetry. Stuffed my metaphors for lunch. Imagination
my cool drink. Empty bag of my stomach blowing tornado,
Frustrated. A gunshot passed through my chest. Another frustration

Publisher's list

If you have enjoyed *A Letter to the President* consider these other fine books from Mwanaka Media and Publishing:

Cultural Hybridity and Fixity by Andrew Nyongesa
The Water Cycle by Andrew Nyongesa
Tintinnabulation of Literary Theory by Andrew Nyongesa
I Threw a Star in a Wine Glass by Fethi Sassi
South Africa and United Nations Peacekeeping Offensive Operations by Antonio Garcia
Africanization and Americanization Anthology Volume 1, Searching for Interracial, Interstitial, Intersectional and Interstates Meeting Spaces, Africa Vs North America by Tendai R Mwanaka
A Conversation..., A Contact by Tendai Rinos Mwanaka
A Dark Energy by Tendai Rinos Mwanaka
Africa, UK and Ireland: Writing Politics and Knowledge Production Vol 1 by Tendai R Mwanaka
Best New African Poets 2017 Anthology by Tendai R Mwanaka and Daniel Da Purificacao
Keys in the River: New and Collected Stories by Tendai Rinos Mwanaka
Logbook Written by a Drifter by Tendai Rinos Mwanaka
Mad Bob Republic: Bloodlines, Bile and a Crying Child by Tendai Rinos Mwanaka
How The Twins Grew Up/Makurire Akaita Mapatya by Milutin Djurickovic and Tendai Rinos Mwanaka
Writing Language, Culture and Development, Africa Vs Asia Vol 1 by Tendai R Mwanaka, Wanjohi wa Makokha and Upal Deb
Zimbolicious Poetry Vol 1 by Tendai R Mwanaka and Edward Dzonze
Zimbolicious: An Anthology of Zimbabwean Literature and Arts, Vol 3 by Tendai Mwanaka
Under The Steel Yoke by Jabulani Mzinyathi
A Case of Love and Hate by Chenjerai Mhondera

Epochs of Morning Light by Elena Botts
Fly in a Beehive by Thato Tshukudu
Bounding for Light by Richard Mbuthia
White Man Walking byJohn Eppel
A Cat and Mouse Affair by Bruno Shora
Sentiments by Jackson Matimba
Best New African Poets 2018 Anthology by Tendai R Mwanaka and Nsah Mala
Drawing Without Licence by Tendai R Mwanaka
Writing Grandmothers/Escribiendo sobre nuestras raíces:Africa Vs Latin America Vol 2 by Tendai R Mwanaka and Felix Rodriguez
The Scholarship Girl by Abigail George
Words That Matter by Gerry Sikazwe
The Gods Sleep Through It by Wonder Guchu
The Ungendered by Delia Watterson
The Big Noise and Other Noises by Christopher Kudyahakudadirwe
Tiny Human Protection Agency by Megan Landman
Ghetto Symphony by Mandla Mavolwane
Sky for a Foreign Bird by Fethi Sassi
A Portrait of Defiance by Tendai Rinos Mwanaka
When Escape Becomes the only Lover by Tendai R Mwanaka
Where I Belong: moments, mist and song by Smeetha Bhoumik

Soon to be released
Of Bloom Smoke by Abigail George
Denga reshiri yokunze kwenyika by Fethi Sassi
Nationalism: (Mis)Understanding   Donald Trump's Capitalism, Racism, Global Politics, International Trade and Media Wars, Africa Vs North America Vol 2 by Tendai R Mwanaka
Ashes by Ken Weene and Umar O. Abdul
Ouafa and Thawra: About a Lover From Tunisia by Arturo Desimone
Thoughts Hunt The Loves/Pfungwa Dzinovhima Vadiwa by Jeton Kelmendi
ويَسهَرُ اللَّيلُ عَلَى شَفَتي...وَالغَمَامُ by Fethi Sassi

Litany of a Foreign Wife by Nnane Ntube
Righteous Indignation by Jabulani Mzinyathi:
Notes From a Modern Chimurenga: Collected Stories by Tendai Rinos Mwanaka:
Tom Boy by Megan Landman
My Spiritual Journey: A Study of the Emerald Tablets by Jonathan Thompson

https://facebook.com/MwanakaMediaAndPublishing/

Printed in the United States
By Bookmasters